T0198761

There's a lizard in my lunchbox

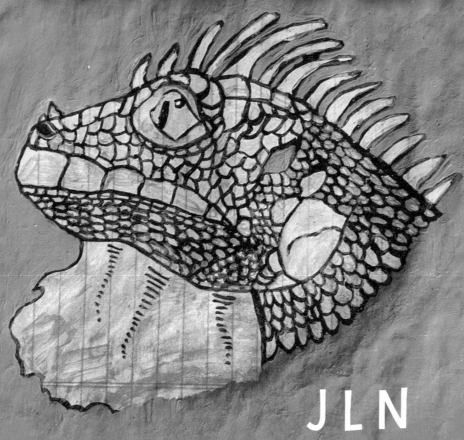

JLN

AuthorHouse™
1663 Liberty Drive
Bloomington, IN 47403
www.authorhouse.com
Phone: 1 (800) 839-8640

This book is printed on acid-free paper.

ISBN: 978-1-7283-4244-3 (sc)
ISBN: 978-1-7283-4245-0 (e)

Print information available on the last page.

Published by AuthorHouse 01/10/2020

author HOUSE®

There's a
lizard
in my
lunchbox

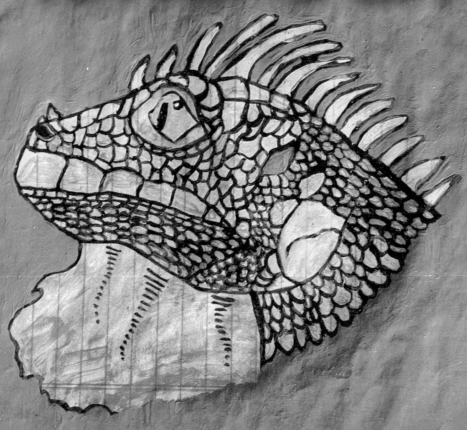

There's a Lizard in my Lunchbox,
her name is Quasi and she's green.

She's always nice and never mean
she is big and has a long tail,
she's my best friend without fail.

There's a Lizard in my Lunchbox,
eating all my food,

She's cunning as a fox,
what am I to do?

She has five fingers and five toes,
scales cover her from tip of tail,
to the tip of her nose.

There's a Lizard in my Lunchbox,
my teacher doesn't know.

She ate right through my cracker box,
now she's going to grow.

How can she fit inside?

She loves to tag along,
she loves to take the ride,

On the bus and off to school,
all my friends think she's really cool.

They like to bring her treats,
its scary how much she eats.

What does she see with her
big golden eyes?
Why its my yummy carrots that she spies.

There's a lizard in my Lunchbox,
I can only see her tail.

There's a Lizard in my Lunchbox,
and I love her each and every scale.

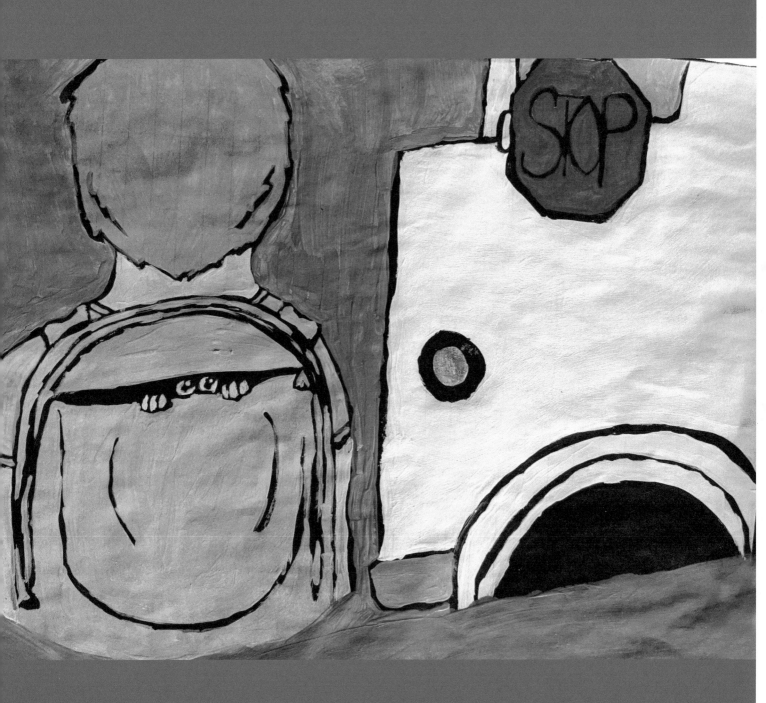

The author wrote this as a way to tell the story of her experience with quasi on her daily adventures to school. Here you will find her exploits through her school day where she taught children what it means to have an iguana as a friend.

Printed in the United States
By Bookmasters